The Rights of the Prophet's Household {Ahlul-Bayt}

Ibn Taymiyyah

Translated & Comments by Al Reshah

Alreshah.net

Canada

Copyright © 2018 by **Alreshah**

All rights reserved. No part of this publication may be reproduced, distributed or transmitted in any form or by any means, without prior written permission.

Alreshah
www.Alreshah.net

Publisher's Note: This is translation of book without change of meaning as best as the translator could achieve with few comments in the footnote to clarify If any error is found please contact us through our website alreshah.net.

Book Layout © 2017 BookDesignTemplates.com

The Rights of the Prophet's Household
{Ahlul-Bayt}/ Ibn Taymiyyah. -- 1st ed.
ISBN 978-1-7753434-6-2

The Book is a Translation and reflect the views of the author and not
Al Rehsah

Footnotes: Mohammad Ahmad

Contents

Introduction 1

Unifying the Muslim Community through the Holy Qur'an and Sunnah 3

The Prophet's Household and their Attributes 11

Their Rights and Duties 17

The Attributes of the Beneficiaries of Gains without War 19

Prohibition of Cursing the Companions on Behalf of the Prophet's Household as well as Others 21

The Shiite's Ignorance with the Doctrine of Imam Ali 27

The Factors of Deviation from What is Right 33

People of the Right Course .... During Calamity 45

Erroneous Innovations and Deviations 53

• CHAPTER 1 •

Introduction

This book addresses the faithful brothers whose wholehearted allegiance belongs entirely to God and His Messenger and to the believers; those who observe their prayers, pay their zakat (purifying alms), and bow down in worship. And whoever is an ally of God and His Messenger and the believers, those who owe their allegiance to the party of God, will indeed be the predominant. It addresses those who harbor genuine love in their hearts towards God and His Messenger and are reciprocated, in return, similar love and those who acknowledge the true stature of the Prophet's Companions as ordained by God and His Messenger. Love and obedience to God entail love and obedience to His Messenger which subsequently entail love for those whom the Prophet had endowed with his love, and obedience to those whom he enjoined to be obeyed.

{يَا أَيُّهَا ٱلَّذِينَ آمَنُوا أَطِيعُوا ٱللَّهَ وَأَطِيعُوا ٱلرَّسُولَ وَأُولِي ٱلْأَمْرِ مِنكُمْ فَإِن تَنَازَعْتُمْ فِي شَيْءٍ فَرُدُّوهُ إِلَى ٱللَّهِ وَٱلرَّسُولِ إِن كُنتُمْ تُؤْمِنُونَ بِٱللَّهِ وَٱلْيَوْمِ ٱلْآخِرِ ذَٰلِكَ خَيْرٌ وَأَحْسَنُ تَأْوِيلًا} (النساء: 59)

O you who have believed, obey Allah and obey the Messenger and those in authority among you. And if you disagree over anything, refer it to Allah and the Messenger, if you should believe in Allah and the Last Day. That is the best [way] and best in result. (An-Nissa':59)

The Prophet (peace be upon him) said, "Whoever obeys me, obeys Allah, and whoever disobeys me, disobeys Allah, and whoever obeys the ruler I appoint, obeys me, and whoever disobeys him, disobeys me."[2] (Al-Bukhari)

On the authority of Prince of the Faithful, Ali ibn Abi Talib that the Prophet was quoted saying, "Conscious obedience is only in that which is good". [3]

And his saying, "No obedience should be offered to a created being in disobedience to the Creator." [4]

May the peace, mercy, and blessings of God be upon you; Praise be to Allah the One and Supreme Lord, Worthy of all Praise, the Able and the Powerful and we supplicate God to exalt the exemplar of righteousness and the seal of prophets, Mohammad (peace be upon Him).

CHAPTER 2

Unifying the Muslim Community through the Holy Qur'an and Sunnah

God has imparted His Revelation and Wisdom unto Mohammad to guide mankind out of darkness into the light by His permission - to the path of the Almighty, the Praiseworthy.

God, Exalted is He, had said,

{لقَدْ مَنَّ اللهُ عَلَى الْمُؤْمِنِينَ إِذْ بَعَثَ فِيهِمْ رَسُولاً مِنْ أَنفُسِهِمْ يَتْلُو عَلَيْهِمْ آيَاتِهِ وَيُزَكِّيهِمْ وَيُعَلِّمُهُمُ الْكِتَابَ وَالْحِكْمَةَ وَإِن كَانُوا مِن قَبْلُ لَفِي ضَلالٍ مُبِينٍ} (آل عمران: 164)

Certainly did Allah confer [great] favor upon the believers when He sent among them a Messenger from themselves, reciting to them His verses and purifying them and teaching them the Book and wisdom, although they had been before in manifest error. (Al-Imran: 164) [5]

He also cited,

{وَاذْكُرُوا نِعْمَتَ اللهِ عَلَيْكُمْ وَمَا أَنزَلَ عَلَيْكُم مِّنَ الْكِتَابِ وَالْحِكْمَةِ يَعِظُكُم بِهِ} (البقرة: 231)

And remember the favor of Allah upon you and what has been revealed to you of the Book and wisdom by which He instructs you. (Al-Baqara: 231)

God had addressed the wives of the Prophet saying,

{وَاذْكُرْنَ مَا يُتْلَىٰ فِي بُيُوتِكُنَّ مِنْ آيَاتِ اللهِ وَالْحِكْمَةِ ۚ إِنَّ اللَّهَ كَانَ لَطِيفًا خَبِيرًا} (الأحزاب: 34)

And remember what is recited in your houses of the verses of Allah and wisdom. Indeed, Allah is ever Subtle and Acquainted [with all things]. (Al-Ahzab: 34)

Through the Prophet's recitation, God has bestowed the book and wisdom onto the Prophet's wives' households.

The book here means the Qur'an; whereas wisdom refers to what the Prophet used to say, i.e. his traditions (sunnah), and hence, Muslims are instructed to learn both.

THE RIGHTS OF THE PROPHET'S HOUSEHOLD {AHLUL-BAYT}

In a famous Hadith narrated by at-Tirmidhi and others on the authority of Prince of the Faithful, Ali ibn Abi Talib, "There will come a time of confusing turmoil!" So I said: "What is the way out, O Messenger of Allah?" He said: "Observe the Book of God! It will acquaint you with accounts of the previous nations, news of the following nations, and resolution for the disputes that occur between you. It is a book of decisive rulings, not an object of ridicule. Whoever forsakes it, however powerful, God will crush him. And whoever seeks guidance apart from it, God will leave him astray. It is the firm rope of religion, the guiding revelation, and the straight path of God. It is not prone to capricious inclinations or twists of tongues. Despite numerous arguments and various denials, it cannot be refuted and will remain ever-revealing. Whoever speaks according to it has said the truth; whoever acts according to it is rewarded; whoever judges by it has ruled justly, and whoever calls people for it has guided them to the straight path."

God has revealed in His Book,

وَاعْتَصِمُوا بِحَبْلِ اللَّهِ جَمِيعًا وَلَا تَفَرَّقُوا (آل عمران: 103)

And hold firmly to the rope of Allah all together and do not become divided. (Al-Imran: 103)

He also proclaimed,

إِنَّ الَّذِينَ فَرَّقُوا دِينَهُمْ وَكَانُوا شِيَعًا لَسْتَ مِنْهُمْ فِي شَيْءٍ (الأنعام: 159)

Indeed, those who have divided their religion and become sects - you, [O Muhammad], are not [associated] with them in anything. (Al-Ana'am: 159) [10]

God has condemned those who were split into groups and sects over their faith, and praised those who followed the true religion of God which is His Book and aligned their faith with the one and only creed of all God's messengers.

وَإِنَّ مِن شِيعَتِهِ لَإِبْرَاهِيمَ (الصافات: 83)

And indeed, among his kind was Abraham. [As Saffat:11]

Abraham is the chief of the prophets as depicted by God,

وَإِذِ ابْتَلَىٰ إِبْرَاهِيمَ رَبُّهُ بِكَلِمَاتٍ فَأَتَمَّهُنَّ قَالَ إِنِّي جَاعِلُكَ لِلنَّاسِ إِمَامًا قَالَ وَمِن ذُرِّيَّتِي قَالَ لَا يَنَالُ عَهْدِي الظَّالِمِينَ (البقرة: 124)

And [mention, O Muhammad], when Abraham was tried by his Lord with commands and he fulfilled them. [Allah] said, "Indeed, I will make you a leader for the people." [Abraham] said, "And of my descendants?" [Allah] said, "My covenant does not include the wrongdoers. (Al-Baqara: 124)

In this regard, He also stated,

THE RIGHTS OF THE PROPHET'S HOUSEHOLD {AHLUL-BAYT}

إنّ إِبْرَاهِيمَ كَانَ أُمَّةً قَانِتًا لِلَّهِ حَنِيفًا وَلَمْ يَكُ مِنَ الْمُشْرِكِينَ (النحل: 120)

Indeed, Abraham was a [comprehensive] leader, devoutly obedient to Allah, inclining toward truth, and he was not of those who associate others with Allah. (An-Nahl: 120)

until saying,

ثُمَّ أَوْحَيْنَا إِلَيْكَ أَنِ اتَّبِعْ مِلَّةَ إِبْرَاهِيمَ حَنِيفًا وَمَا كَانَ مِنَ الْمُشْرِكِينَ (النحل: 123)

Then We revealed to you, [O Muhammad], to follow the religion of Abraham, inclining toward truth; and he was not of those who associate with Allah. (An-Nahl: 123)

The Prophet has taught his nation to say at daybreak, "We begin our morning maintaining the natural constitution of Islam, holding to sincere faith, and acknowledging the true religion of our Prophet Mohammad (peace be upon him) and the creed of our father, Abraham, who turned away from all that was false and was not one of those who associated partners with God." [1]

The Prophet proclaimed, "Indeed, God has entrusted me with the revelation of His Book and the like of it. It is as if there is a man, his stomach full, lounging on his couch and saying, 'Stick with the Qur'an. What you find permissible in it consider it permitted; and what you find prohibited in it, consider it

---

[1] Musnad Ahmad, Al Nasai ,

prohibited'. But God has entrusted me with the revelation of His Book and the like of it." [2]

This hadith is in accordance with God's Revelation stating that the Prophet (peace be upon him) will recite God's revelations and wisdom which he was given from on high together with the book.

In His Book, God had ordained Muslims to hold onto the firm rope of religion and forbidden their disagreement and division. He enjoined us to stick to one creed and not divide to different sects. God stated in His book,

وَإِن طَائِفَتَانِ مِنَ الْمُؤْمِنِينَ اقْتَتَلُوا فَأَصْلِحُوا بَيْنَهُمَا ۖ فَإِن بَغَتْ إِحْدَاهُمَا عَلَى الْأُخْرَىٰ فَقَاتِلُوا الَّتِي تَبْغِي حَتَّىٰ تَفِيءَ إِلَىٰ أَمْرِ اللَّهِ ۚ فَإِن فَاءَتْ فَأَصْلِحُوا بَيْنَهُمَا بِالْعَدْلِ وَأَقْسِطُوا ۖ إِنَّ اللَّهَ يُحِبُّ الْمُقْسِطِينَ ۰ إِنَّمَا الْمُؤْمِنُونَ إِخْوَةٌ فَأَصْلِحُوا بَيْنَ أَخَوَيْكُمْ ۚ وَاتَّقُوا اللَّهَ لَعَلَّكُمْ تُرْحَمُونَ (الحجرات: 9-10)

And if two factions among the believers should fight, then make settlement between the two. But if one of them oppresses the other, then fight against the one that oppresses until it returns to the ordinance of Allah. And if it returns, then make settlement between them in justice and act justly. Indeed, Allah loves those who act justly. The believers are but brothers, so make settlement between your brothers.

---

[2] Ibn Majah, Musnad Ahmad

THE RIGHTS OF THE PROPHET'S HOUSEHOLD {AHLUL-BAYT}

And fear Allah that you may receive mercy. (Al-Hujurat: 9-10)

God had intended Muslims to be brothers and enjoined them to make just settlements should fight or oppression occur between them.

A hadith quoted the Prophet as saying, "The similitude of believers in regard to mutual love, affection, and compassion is that of one body; when any limb of it aches, the whole-body aches out of sleeplessness and fever." [3]

And said, "The bond of a believer to his brother believer is like a firm structure, enforcing each other." He illustrated this by interlacing the fingers of both his hands. [4]

Such are the origins of Islam: the book and wisdom. It is a prerequisite for all believers to hold fast to the firm rope of religion to remain steadfast in their faith.

---

[3] Al Bukhari
[4] Al Bukhari

• CHAPTER 3 •

The Prophet's Household and their Attributes

Who are the members of the Prophet's Household?

No doubt, God had imparted an aura of sanctity upon the Prophet's household just like the one due to the Caliphs, the vanguards of faith, and their followers in benefaction.

God Almighty had said,

يَا أَيُّهَا النَّبِيُّ قُل لِأَزْوَاجِكَ إِن كُنتُنَّ تُرِدْنَ الْحَيَاةَ الدُّنْيَا وَزِينَتَهَا فَتَعَالَيْنَ أُمَتِّعْكُنَّ وَأُسَرِّحْكُنَّ سَرَاحًا جَمِيلًا. وَإِن كُنتُنَّ تُرِدْنَ اللَّهَ وَرَسُولَهُ وَالدَّارَ الْآخِرَةَ فَإِنَّ اللَّهَ أَعَدَّ لِلْمُحْسِنَاتِ مِنكُنَّ أَجْرًا عَظِيمًا. (الأحزاب: 28- 29)

O Prophet, say to your wives, "If you should desire the worldly life and its adornment, then come, I will provide for you and give you a gracious release. But if you should desire

Allah and His Messenger and the home of the Hereafter - then indeed, Allah has prepared for the doers of good among you a great reward. (Al-Ahzab: 28)

Imam Ahmad and at-Titmidhi narrated on the authority of Um-Salama: when this verse was revealed, the Prophet wrapped Ali, Fatima, al-Hassan, and al-Hussein (may God be pleased with them) in his cloak and said, "O Allah! These are the members of my household; remove from them the impurity of sin and purify them with thorough purification."

Needless to say, the Prophet's sayings and practices (sunnah) illustrate, elaborate, and interpret the book of God.

So, although the Qur'anic context refers to the Prophet's wives as his household, it is apparent from the Prophet's saying (members of my household) that his kin are more entitled to be his household, for blood relationship is much stronger than lineage through matrimony.

For Arabs, such declaration implies the notion of thoroughness rather than exclusiveness. In a similar context, the Prophet had reported,

"A pauper is not the one who goes from door to door begging for a morsel or two or a date or two. But a pauper is the one who has no means of support and does not reveal his destituteness to others so that he might be given charity and is ashamed to beg from others." [5]

THE RIGHTS OF THE PROPHET'S HOUSEHOLD {AHLUL-BAYT}

Accordingly, the hadith here refers to thorough paragraph, for the wanderer who goes from door to door begging, though still a pauper is not a thorough one because he is sometimes given charity.

It is said: this is the scholar, this is the enemy, this is the Muslim when he possesses the thorough attributes to declare him so, though others might share these attributes in a lesser way.

In a similar hadith mentioned in Sahih Muslim, the Prophet had been asked about the mosque that had been founded on piety, he answered, "my mosque", meaning the Mosque of Medina, even though the Qur'anic context, when speaking of the mosque that had been established out of mischievous motives, implies that the mosque that had been founded on piety is that of Qibba'.

لاَ تَقُمْ فِيهِ أَبَدًا لَمَسْجِدٌ أُسِّسَ عَلَى التَّقْوَىٰ مِنْ أَوَّلِ يَوْمٍ أَحَقُّ أَنْ تَقُومَ فِيهِ فِيهِ رِجَالٌ يُحِبُّونَ أَنْ يَتَطَهَّرُوا وَاللَّهُ يُحِبُّ الْمُطَّهِّرِينَ (التوبة: 108)

Do not stand [for prayer] within it - ever. A mosque founded on righteousness from the first day is more worthy for you to stand in. Within it are men who love to purify themselves; and Allah loves those who purify themselves. (At-Tawbah: 108)

---

[5] Al Bukhari

It had been reported that the Prophet asked the people of Qibba', "What kind of purification do you perform for which God has praised you? They said, 'We clean ourselves with water (after relieving themselves).'"[6]

Accordingly, though both are founded on piety, the Prophet's Mosque is more entitled to be founded on piety more than the mosque of Qibba' and more entitled for establishing prayers.

It was reported that the Prophet (peace be upon him) used to come up to Qibba' every Saturday, either riding or on foot. Thus, he would perform the Friday Congregation Prayer in his mosque and offer prayers in Qibba' on Saturday[7], both mosques being founded on piety.

Therefore, when God Almighty declared that He wanted to remove all impurity from the household of the Prophet, the latter (peace be upon him) called his closest and most special kin: Ali and Fatima (may God be pleased with them) together with the most notable youth of Paradise. God had endowed them with two things: means of purification and the immaculate supplication of the Prophet. So, it was out of God's mercy and grace, not their strength or capability, that God had removed all impurity from them. If the reverse were true, they would have accomplished it without the Prophet's supplication; people

---

[6] Musnad ahmad
[7] Al Bukhari

THE RIGHTS OF THE PROPHET'S HOUSEHOLD {AHLUL-BAYT}

would then think that they could be directed to guidance and piety without God's aid or support.

It has been reported through authorized transmission that when these verses were revealed, the Prophet recited them to his wives and offered them to choose, as dictated by God. They chose God, His Messenger, and the life to come, and so the Prophet retained them and did not divorce them until his death. Had they favored worldly luxuries and adornments, he would have released them in a gracious manner as dictated by god, for he was (peace be upon him) the most pious and most observable of God's limits.

Regarding what these verses suggest of doubling the reward as well as doubling the punishment, it was reported that Imam Ali ibn al-Hussein Zein al-Abedeen, the apple of the Muslims' eyes, had said, "I hope that the beneficent among us would be rewarded twice, but also fear lest the offender among us should bear double punishment."

It was reported in Sahih Muslim on the authority of Zayd ibn Arqam that he said: one day the Messenger of Allah (peace be upon him) delivered a sermon at a watering place known as Khumm between Mecca and Medina. He said, "Attend to your duties toward the members of my household. Attend to your duties toward the members of my household. Zayd ibn Arqam was asked, "Who are the members of his household?" Thereupon Zayd said, "Those who are forbidden to receive charity: the house of Ali, the house of 'Aqil, the house of Ja'far, and the house of Abbas." Zayd was asked, "Are all these among the Prophet's household?" He said, "Yes".

When this verse was revealed through authentic transmission,

إنّ اللَّهَ وَمَلَائِكَتَهُ يُصَلُّونَ عَلَى النَّبِيِّ يَا أَيُّهَا الَّذِينَ آمَنُوا صَلُّوا عَلَيْهِ وَسَلِّمُوا تَسْلِيمًا (الأحزاب: 56)

Indeed, Allah confers blessing upon the Prophet, and His angels [ask Him to do so]. O you who have believed, ask [Allah to confer] blessing upon him and ask [Allah to grant him] peace. (Al-Ahzab: 56)

the Companions asked how they could pray for him. He said, "Say: O God! Exalt Mohammad and the people of Mohammad, as You exalted Abraham and the people of Abraham. You are the All Praiseworthy and the All Glorious.
Another verified version quotes, "O God! Exalt Mohammad, his wives, and his offspring." [8]

---

[8] Al Bukhari

• CHAPTER 4 •

Their Rights and Duties

It was reported that when his grandson, al-Hassan ibn Ali took one date from the dates assigned to charity and put it in his mouth, the Prophet said, "Expel it from your mouth. Don't you know that we do not eat a thing which is given in charity?" [9]

He also said, "Charity is not permissible for Mohammad or for his household." [10]

This ruling -God knows best- falls under the assurance of purging the Prophet's household as prescribed by God. Charity purifies the filth of people; hence God has refined them from being liable to such filth and compensated them with one-fifth of war gains as well as with allocations of gains achieved without war as means of subsistence. In this regard, the Prophet had said, in a narration by Ahmad and others, "I was sent

---

[9] Al Bukhari
[10] Musnad Ahmad

accompanied by the sword before the Hour until God is worshipped with no other partners. My livelihood was allocated under the shade of my spear. Whoever disobeys me in this matter will be humiliated by paying Jizya and whoever mimics a group of people is counted amongst them." [11]

Therefore, it is the duty of the Muslim community to take care of providing adequate means of subsistence for the Prophet's household, considering they are not allowed to take charity, more than providing for others in charity, especially when it becomes unfeasible to give them their one-fifth share of war gains or their allocation of gains without war: either out of deficiency or out of usurpation of their rights by unjust rulers. In this case, they can be given allocations from charity to compensate the deficiency in their one-fifth share or their allocation of the free gains.

---

[11] Musnad Ahmad

• CHAPTER 5 •

The Attributes of the Beneficiaries of Gains without War

The attributes of those who are singled out as the beneficiaries of gains without war from kinsfolk and others are highlighted in God's Revelations by saying,

مَّا أَفَاءَ اللَّهُ عَلَىٰ رَسُولِهِ مِنْ أَهْلِ الْقُرَىٰ فَلِلَّهِ وَلِلرَّسُولِ وَلِذِي الْقُرْبَىٰ وَالْيَتَامَىٰ وَالْمَسَاكِينِ وَابْنِ السَّبِيلِ (الحشر:7)

And what Allah restored to His Messenger from the people of the towns - it is for Allah and for the Messenger and for [his] near relatives and orphans and the [stranded] traveler (Al-Hashr: 7)

So, the beneficiaries of the gains without war are divided into three groups: al-Muhajirin, al-Ansar, and the later generations who follow in their footsteps and say: Our Lord, forgive us and our brothers who preceded us in faith and put not in our hearts [any] resentment toward those who have believed. Our Lord, indeed You are Kind and Merciful.

Such gains (without war) were only achieved through al-Muhajirin and al-Ansar's hard strife, faith, migration, and support. Later generations gain possession of them in succession, just like a son inheriting his father provided he holds the same faith, for "an infidel cannot inherit a Muslim". [12]

Accordingly, those who do not ask God to forgive al-Muhajirin and al-Ansar and those who harbor grudge in their hearts towards them are excluded from being among the beneficiaries of gains without war as described by God until their hearts acknowledge their privilege and their tongue pray for them. Should any of them commit a grave transgression, God would forgive it owing to their numerous good deeds, true repentance, infliction with a purging hardship, acceptance of the Prophet's or believers' intercession, or in answer for their prayers.

---

[12] Al Bukhari

• CHAPTER 6 •

Prohibition of Cursing the Companions on Behalf of the Prophet's Household as well as Others

It was authentically reported on the authority of the Prince of the Faithful Ali ibn Abi Talib RA that Hatib ibn Abi Balta' wrote to the infidels of Mecca briefing them with the Prophet's intention to conquer it and dispatched this piece of information with a traveling woman. The Revelation warned the Prophet (peace be upon him) so he sent Ali and Zubair on her heels and they were able to fetch the letter. The Prophet said, "O Hatib! What made you do this?" Hatib replied, "O Messenger of Allah! I swear to God that I did not do this out of disbelief or intending harm. I was a person not belonging to Quraysh but I was an ally of them from outside and had no blood relation with them, and all the Emigrants who were with you, have got their kinsmen (in

Mecca) who can protect their families and properties. So I liked to do them a favor so that they might protect my relatives as I have no blood relation there." Omar said, "O Allah's Messenger! Let me chop off the head of this hypocrite!" The Prophet said, "He (i.e. Hatib) has witnessed the battle of Badr and what do you know, perhaps God looked upon the veterans of Badr and said, "O veterans of Badr, do whatever you like, for I have forgiven you." The following verses were consequently revealed:

يَا أَيُّهَا الَّذِينَ آمَنُوا لَا تَتَّخِذُوا عَدُوِّي وَعَدُوَّكُمْ أَوْلِيَاءَ تُلْقُونَ إِلَيْهِم بِالْمَوَدَّةِ (الممتحنة: 1)

O you who have believed, do not take My enemies and your enemies as allies, extending to them affection (Al-Mumtahanah: 1)

It was reported in Sahih Muslim that a slave of Hatib came to the Messenger of Allah (peace be upon him) complaining about Hatib, saying: 'O Messenger of Allah! Hatib will definitely go to Hell!' because Hatib used to ill-treat his slaves. So the Prophet said: 'You have lied! No one who had participated in the battle of Badr and the pledge of allegiance at al-Hudaybiyah would enter it.'" He also said, "Whoever pledged his allegiance under the tree would not enter Hell." [13]

---

[13] Al Tarmithe

THE RIGHTS OF THE PROPHET'S HOUSEHOLD {AHLUL-BAYT}

Despite his grave transgression which was sending a dispatch to the people of Mecca when the Prophet wanted to keep the people there in the dark regarding his true objective and despite his ill-treatment of his slaves: in the traceable hadith, "an abusive master would not enter Paradise", God had forgiven him and was even pleased with him on the grounds of being a veteran of Badr and pledging his allegiance at al-Hudaybiyah, for good deeds obliterate bad ones.

So, how about those who are better than Hatib, more faithful, knowledgeable, and are the antecedents of migration, who never came near a similar transgression?

The Prince of the Faithful, Ali ibn Abi Talib, related the previously mentioned hadith during his caliphate which was narrated by his scribe, Obaidullah ibn Abi Rafi'. He stated that he and Zubair had tracked down the traveling woman to demand the letter. Despite the Prince of the Faithful knowledge of what had occurred (on behalf of Hatib), the Prophet had borne witness to the meritorious status of the veterans of Badr in order to prevent hearts and tongues from giving rise to evil talk about his Companions. None of them had committed what Hatib had perpetrated; if so it would be out of independent judgment.

The Prophet (peace be upon him) said, "If a judge gives a verdict according to the best of his knowledge and his verdict is correct (i.e. agrees with Allah and His Apostle's verdict) he will receive a double reward, and if he gives a verdict according to the best of his knowledge and his verdict is wrong, then he will get a single reward." [14]

This is a well-known and authentic hadith.

It was also reported that during the attack of the confederate forces whom God turned back in their rage and fury without gaining any good, God commanded His Prophet to march to the Qurayẓah. So, the Prophet issued an order to all his Companions: "None of you would pray 'Aṣr (the afternoon prayer) except at the Qurayẓah."

On their way, the 'Aṣr prayer became due. Some of them said: we won't pray except when we arrive at the Qurayẓah; others stopped to offer it arguing that the Prophet had only wanted them to start marching immediately. The Prophet blamed neither party.

This attitude of the Prophet comes in accordance with what God stated in his book:

وَدَاوُودَ وَسُلَيْمَانَ إِذْ يَحْكُمَانِ فِي الْحَرْثِ إِذْ نَفَشَتْ فِيهِ غَنَمُ الْقَوْمِ وَكُنَّا لِحُكْمِهِمْ شَاهِدِينَ فَفَهَّمْنَاهَا سُلَيْمَانَ وَكُلًّا آتَيْنَا حُكْمًا وَعِلْمًا (الأحزاب: 78-79)

And [mention] David and Solomon, when they judged concerning the field - when the sheep of a people overran it

---

[14] Al Bukhari

[at night], and We were witness to their judgment. And We gave understanding of the case to Solomon, and to each [of them] We gave judgment and knowledge.

(al-Ahzab: 78-79)

God elaborated that He had endowed one of the two prophets with a sound judgment in this issue, while He praised both for the knowledge and judgment they had been given.

In this manner, the vanguards who took the lead among the Muhājirīn and the Anṣār, as well as those who followed in their footsteps, with whom God is well-pleased and well-pleased are they with Him used juristic deduction in their arguments seeking that which is right.

CHAPTER 7

The Shiite's Ignorance with the Doctrine of Imam Ali

The Prophet (peace be upon him) said, "Indeed, whoever among you lives after me, will see great disagreement. You must then follow my sunnah and that of the rightly-guided caliphs. Hold to it and stick fast to it. Avoid novelties, for every novelty is an innovation, and every innovation leads astray."[15]

Safinah narrated that the Prophet had said, "The Caliphate system lasts thirty years and then transforms into monarchy." [16]The thirty years terminated when the Prophet's grandson, al-Hassan ibn Ali (may God be pleased with them both) transferred the authority to Muawiyah.

---

[15] Musnad Ahmad
[16] Musnad Ahmad

Muawiyah was the first monarch and he was merciful, as stated in the hadith, "It will be a Caliphate of prophecy, then merciful monarchy, then oppressive monarchy, and then relentless monarchy."[17]

It was related that when the Prince of the Faithful, Ali ibn Abi Talib (may Allah be pleased with him) fought against the people of the camel, he did not curse their descendants, take their possessions as booty, kill the injured, chase down the escapees, or execute the captives. He prayed for the dead of both parties in the battle of the Camel and Siffin. He used to say, "Our brethren have wronged us."

He also said that they were neither considered unbelievers or hypocrites and he judged them in the light of the Qur'an and sunnah. God had called them brethren and they retained the attribute of being believers despite their fighting and transgressing against each other.

وَإِن طَائِفَتَانِ مِنَ الْمُؤْمِنِينَ اقْتَتَلُوا

And if two factions among the believers should fight [Al-Hujurat :47]

It was quoted with verified authorization that the Prophet said, "A group will secede in a time of dissension among

---

[17] Abi Dawood

Muslims. Out of the two groups which is closer to the truth will kill them."[18]

The seceding group were the people of Harora' who were killed at the hands of the Prince of the Faithful, Ali ibn Abi Talib when they apostatized, revolted against him, accused him and the rest of the Muslims with infidelity, and even considered the other members of the Muslim community proscribed individuals.

It was reported, according to continuous lines of transmission, that the Prophet had described them and gave orders to fight them, saying, "If anyone of you compares his prayer with theirs, he will consider his prayer, his fasting, and his recitation of the Qur'an inferior to theirs. They would recite the Qur'an but it would not go beyond their collar-bones, for in fact they are abandoning Islam so hurriedly just like an arrow being shot from its bow. If those who are commissioned to kill them realize what reward awaits them as declared by Mohammad (peace be upon him), they would forsake all other good deeds.[19]

Hence, they were fought by Ali (may God be pleased with him) and his companions and he was immensely satisfied with this accomplishment that he prostrated in gratitude to God. There was a consensus of the Companions' opinion about the

---

[18] Muslim
[19] Al Bukhari

lawfulness of fighting them, especially when their manifest signs began to show up: a man with a crippled hand and flesh-like arm with few hairs thereon. Many Companions, including Ibn Omar and others, regretted the fact that they did not participate in such combat, unlike the Battle of the Camel and Siffin where the Prince of the Faithful was so unwilling to fight and lamented the complexity of the situation. Many a time his son, al-Hassan argued with him about its lawfulness, the former's opinion being against it.

Accordingly, what satisfied the Prince of the Faithful and his companions and aroused the regret of those who did not participate while bearing in mind what the Prophet had said in this regard is not equal to what weighed heavily on his heart, being the cherished one to the Prophet who said regarding Ali, "O Allah, behold, I love him. You too love him and love the one who loves him."

The Prince of the faithful was amongst the party closer to the truth than the opposing one in all his battles.

The casualties for whom he prayed and designated as brethren cannot be equal to those for whom he refrained from praying. Rather, when asked who were the ones whose labor in this world has been misguided, and who nonetheless think that what they do is right, he said: the people of Harora'.

THE RIGHTS OF THE PROPHET'S HOUSEHOLD {AHLUL-BAYT}

This disparity which the Prince of the Faithful identified between the people of Harora' and others through word and deed and in accordance with the Qur'an and sunnah was the unequivocal and truly guided right which many predecessor and successor scholars failed to perceive. Rather, they put all on the same level while writing historical literature.

They either fall short in demonstrating the hatred, curse, punishment, and execution due to the Kharijites or assign others more than they deserve in condemnation.

• CHAPTER 8 •

The Factors of Deviation from What is Right

Factors of deviation include lack of knowledge and understanding of God's Revelations, the Prophet's authorized sunnah, and the historical literature of the rightly-guided Caliphs. Otherwise, those who seek the guidance and support of God track down authorized transmission and contemplate the Qur'anic passages and the sunnah of the Prophet and of his caliphs, particularly the historical literature of the Prince of the Faithful[20], the rightly guided and guiding rightly. The confusing ambiguity of his literature caused many people to deviate either in overestimation or aversion.

---

[20] He means Ali Ibn Abi Talib

He once said, "Two men will perish because of me: a loving extremist who overestimates my praise and an antagonist who dubs me with what God has absolved me of." [21]

The means by which man can discern between the two contrary situations is seeking guidance and avoiding subjective inclinations so that he would not be misguided or misled, but rightly guided and insightful.

وَالنَّجْمِ إِذَا هَوَىٰ مَا ضَلَّ صَاحِبُكُمْ وَمَا غَوَىٰ وَمَا يَنطِقُ عَنِ الْهَوَىٰ إِنْ هُوَ إِلَّا وَحْيٌ يُوحَىٰ (النجم: 1-4)

By the star when it descends, our companion [Muhammad] has not strayed, nor has he erred, Nor does he speak from [his own] inclination. It is not but a revelation revealed (An-Najm: 1-4)

The Prophet was not described as being led astray, meaning ignorant, or misleading, meaning transgressor. Once man recognizes the truth and adheres to it by word and deed, righteousness becomes feasible. Whoever remains ignorant of the truth is misguided; whereas whoever recognizes but contradicts it and follows whimsical inclinations is misled. Whoever entertains the truth by word and deed possesses

---

[21] Musnad Ahmad

strength and religious vision. It is the straight path that God ordained to follow in every prayer saying,

اهْدِنَا الصِّرَاطَ المُسْتَقِيمَ صِرَاطَ الذِينَ أَنْعَمْتَ عَلَيْهِمْ غَيْرِ المَغْضُوبِ عَلَيْهِمْ وَلَا الضَّالِينَ

Guide us to the straight path -The path of those upon whom You have bestowed favor, not of those who have evoked [Your] anger or of those who are astray. Al Fatiha 6&7

Those who have earned God's anger are those to whom truth is evident, nevertheless, they do not willfully follow it like the Jews. Those who are astray are those who harbor good intentions in their hearts and labor with their hands but in vain due to lack of knowledge. So God depicts the Jews as misleading by saying,

سَأَصْرِفُ عَنْ آيَاتِيَ الَّذِينَ يَتَكَبَّرُونَ فِي الْأَرْضِ بِغَيْرِ الْحَقِّ وَإِن يَرَوْا كُلَّ آيَةٍ لَا يُؤْمِنُوا بِهَا وَإِن يَرَوْا سَبِيلَ الرُّشْدِ لَا يَتَّخِذُوهُ سَبِيلاً وَإِن يَرَوْا سَبِيلَ الْغَيِّ يَتَّخِذُوهُ سَبِيلاً (الأعراف: 146)

I will turn away from My signs those who are arrogant upon the earth without right; and if they should see every sign, they will not believe in it. And if they see the way of consciousness, they will not adopt it as a way; but if they see the way of error, they will adopt it as a way. (Al-Araf: 146)

And depicts the scholar who refrains from applying his knowledge in practice as,

وَاتْلُ عَلَيْهِمْ نَبَأَ الَّذِي آتَيْنَاهُ آيَاتِنَا فَانسَلَخَ مِنْهَا فَأَتْبَعَهُ الشَّيْطَانُ فَكَانَ مِنَ الْغَاوِينَ وَلَوْ شِئْنَا لَرَفَعْنَاهُ بِهَا وَلَكِنَّهُ أَخْلَدَ إِلَى الْأَرْضِ وَاتَّبَعَ هَوَاهُ (الأعراف: 175)

And recite to them, [O Muhammad], the news of him to whom we gave [knowledge of] Our signs, but he detached himself from them; so Satan pursued him, and he became of the deviators. And if We had willed, we could have elevated him thereby, but he adhered [instead] to the earth and followed his own desire. (Al-Araf: 175)

He also described Christians as being led astray by saying,

وَلَا تَتَّبِعُوا أَهْوَاءَ قَوْمٍ قَدْ ضَلُّوا مِن قَبْلُ وَأَضَلُّوا كَثِيرًا وَضَلُّوا عَن سَوَاءِ السَّبِيلِ (المائدة: 77)

And do not follow the inclinations of a people who had gone astray before and misled many and have strayed from the soundness of the way. (Al-Ma'ida :77)

God has portrayed those who blindly follow their inclinations without knowledge as,

وَمَا لَكُمْ أَلَّا تَأْكُلُوا مِمَّا ذُكِرَ اسْمُ اللَّهِ عَلَيْهِ وَقَدْ فَصَّلَ لَكُم مَّا حَرَّمَ عَلَيْكُمْ إِلَّا مَا اضْطُرِرْتُمْ إِلَيْهِ وَإِنَّ كَثِيرًا لَّيُضِلُّونَ بِأَهْوَائِهِم بِغَيْرِ عِلْمٍ إِنَّ رَبَّكَ هُوَ أَعْلَمُ بِالْمُعْتَدِينَ (الأنعام: 119)

THE RIGHTS OF THE PROPHET'S HOUSEHOLD {AHLUL-BAYT}

And indeed do many lead [others] astray through their [own] inclinations without knowledge. Indeed, your Lord - He is most knowing of the transgressors. (al an'am : 119)

وَمَنْ أَضَلُّ مِمَّنِ اتَّبَعَ هَوَاهُ بِغَيْرِ هُدًى مِّنَ اللَّهِ (القصص: 50)

And who is more astray than one who follows his desire without guidance from Allah? (Al-Qasas : 50)

He stated that whoever follows guidance from God will never deviate like those who went astray or meet an ill-fate like those who have procured God's wrath.

فَإِمَّا يَأْتِيَنَّكُم مِّنِّي هُدًى فَمَنِ اتَّبَعَ هُدَايَ فَلَا يَضِلُّ وَلَا يَشْقَىٰ (طه: 123)

And if there should come to you guidance from Me - then whoever follows My guidance will neither go astray [in the world] nor suffer [in the Hereafter]. (Taha:123)

Regarding this, ibn Abbas said: God had guaranteed that whoever recites Quran and practices its rulings will neither go astray in this world nor suffer in the Hereafter.

Complete guidance entails that whoever seeks guidance must contemplate the Qur'an and the authentic sunnah of the Prophet, the rightly guided caliphs, and the trustworthy scholars. He should discern between the former reliable sources and those who did not accurately memorize the hadith or forged it for some reason. Whoever cites a forged hadith, does one of two things: he either lies willfully, or lies unintentionally due to bad memorization, forgetfulness, misunderstanding, or unreliable recording.

Having accomplished this stage, the seeker of guidance starts to compare between the authentic and the uncertain to get to know the authentic in essence, however different in details; the most likely to be traced to the Prophet and should be followed; and the least likely in its traceability and cannot be considered evidence, despite its apparent soundness.

As for accidental error, people often fall victims to it when they fail to discern between what is reasonable in the light of texts and antiquities and between what is reasonable in the light of juristic reasoning or sheer considering. When falsehood in knowledge is mingled with personal inclination in practice, the following Qur'anic verse would perfectly fit,

إن يَتَّبِعُونَ إِلاَّ الظَّنَّ وَمَا تَهْوَى الأنفُسُ وَلَقَدْ جَاءَهُم مِّن رَّبِّهِمُ الْهُدَىٰ (النجم: 23)

They follow not except assumption and what [their] souls desire, and there has already come to them from their Lord guidance. (Al Najim : 23)

Human nature encompasses two weaknesses: lack of proper knowledge and lack of justice in practice. The former leads man to follow uncertainties, while the latter leads him to follow

THE RIGHTS OF THE PROPHET'S HOUSEHOLD {AHLUL-BAYT}

inclinations and desires. When God sent His messengers and revealed His books for guiding people, those who took up God's guidance kept enough distance from following this course. God had said,

كَانَ النَّاسُ أُمَّةً وَاحِدَةً فَبَعَثَ اللّهُ النَّبِيِّينَ مُبَشِّرِينَ وَمُنذِرِينَ وَأَنزَلَ مَعَهُمُ الْكِتَابَ بِالْحَقِّ لِيَحْكُمَ بَيْنَ النَّاسِ فِيمَا اخْتَلَفُوا فِيهِ وَمَا اخْتَلَفَ فِيهِ إِلاَّ الَّذِينَ أُوتُوهُ مِن بَعْدِ مَا جَاءتْهُمُ الْبَيِّنَاتُ بَغْيًا بَيْنَهُمْ فَهَدَى اللّهُ الَّذِينَ آمَنُوا لِمَا اخْتَلَفُوا فِيهِ مِنَ الْحَقِّ بِإِذْنِهِ وَاللّهُ يَهْدِي مَن يَشَاءُ إِلَى صِرَاطٍ مُسْتَقِيمٍ (البقرة:213)

Mankind was [of] one religion [before their deviation]; then Allah sent the prophets as bringers of good tidings and warners and sent down with them the Scripture in truth to judge between the people concerning that in which they differed. And none differed over the Scripture except those who were given it - after the clear proofs came to them - out of jealous animosity among themselves. And Allah guided those who believed to the truth concerning that over which they had differed, by (Al Baqaraa:213) **His permission. And Allah guides whom He wills to a straight path.**

This depiction of man by God is not applicable only to non-Muslims, or to a single group of the Muslim community, but when ignorance and injustice hit the origin of faith, in case of non-Muslims, the outcome is utter infidelity and total loss. Therefore, the punishment awaiting those who innovate anything in the origins of religion is more severe than the punishment of those who commit an error in tiny matters.

Needless to say, the human soul is always keen on highlighting its own merits and exposing the demerits of others.

Honest scholars say nothing but the truth and strictly follow it. Therefore, those who follow authentic transmissions of the Prophet (PBUH), his Caliphs, his Companions, and the prominent scholars of the Prophet's household, like Ali ibn al-Hussein Zein al-Abedeen; his son, Abi Ja'afar Mohammad ibn Ali al-Baqir; his son Imam Abi Abdullah Ja'afar ibn Mohammad as-Sadiq, the senior scholar of the Muslim Nation; and like Anas ibn Malik, al-Thawri, and similar scholars, will find these transmissions unified and analogous in the origins of religion and Shariah codes and will find in them what substitutes for and dispenses with the contradicting articles of later generations who harbor enmity to the Prophet's household, underestimate their rights, or wish them harm; or who praise them excessively, lie about them, or undervalue the predecessors' rights. In my opinion, what was transmitted from the predecessors (al salaf) in the chapter of the Oneness and Attributes of God; the chapter of justice and fate; the chapter of faith, names and judgments; the chapter of admonition, reward and punishment; the chapter of enjoining good and forbidding evil and what relates to it of the ruling of governors: the righteous and the wicked, and the ruling of their subjects; and talk about the Companions and kinship manifests that whatever arguments occurred among the predecessors, it was the kind of argument which was approved by the book and sunnah and that the flagrant innovations that contradicted the book and sunnah were introduced by the successors. They even went as far as to attribute them to some predecessors: once through unreliable transmission and another time through arbitrary interpretation of unspecific texts.

However, due to God's grace and mercy, the authentic and reliable transmissions expose their falsehood in transmission and interpretation. This is because the straight path in the entire nation is a path of sovereignty, and the perfection of Islam lies in its moderate approach in religion and sovereignty,

وَكَذَلِكَ جَعَلْنَاكُمْ أُمَّةً وَسَطًا (البقرة: 143)

And thus, we have made you a just community. [Al Baqara :143)

They did not deviate like the Jews, the Christians, and the apostates.

Similarly, upright people held tight to the Prophet's sunnah, the predecessors' guidance, and the moderate religion, and did not go astray.

The Jews for example turned their backs on their messengers and the supporters of truth, disbelieved, and even killed them. God had said in this regard,

فَفَرِيقًا كَذَّبْتُمْ وَفَرِيقًا تَقْتُلُونَ (البقرة: 87)

And a party [of messengers] you denied and another party you killed. [Al Baqara: 87)

Whereas the Christians went to extremes when they worshipped them; God had said in this regard,

يَا أَهْلَ الْكِتَابِ لَا تَغْلُوا فِي دِينِكُمْ وَلَا تَقُولُوا عَلَى اللَّهِ إِلَّا الْحَقَّ (النساء: 171)

O People of the Scripture do not commit excess in your religion or say about Allah except the truth. (Al Nisa: 171)

Moreover, the Jews had deviated regarding abrogation when they assumed that it cannot occur on behalf of God and that it is not allowed. In this regard, God had reprimanded them saying,

سَيَقُولُ السُّفَهَاءُ مِنَ النَّاسِ مَا وَلَّاهُمْ عَنْ قِبْلَتِهِمُ الَّتِي كَانُوا عَلَيْهَا قُلْ لِلَّهِ الْمَشْرِقُ وَالْمَغْرِبُ يَهْدِي مَنْ يَشَاءُ إِلَىٰ صِرَاطٍ مُسْتَقِيمٍ (البقرة: 142)

The foolish among the people will say, "What has turned them away from their qiblah, which they used to face? (Al Baqara: 142)

While the Christians went the other way around when they gave their priests and monks the green light to permit and prohibit whatever they liked. Likewise, they contradicted the Jews in every other aspect.

THE RIGHTS OF THE PROPHET'S HOUSEHOLD {AHLUL-BAYT}

Accordingly, God had guided the believers to moderation: they truly believed in their prophets, reverenced, supported, loved, obeyed, and followed them. They did not turn their backs on them as did the Jews nor did they go to extremes by worshipping them as did the Christians.

Similarly, they approved God's abrogation and did not approve anyone else's, for God maintains supreme command over His creation; He is the Ultimate Sovereign and Supreme Commander.

Likewise, fair Muslims who adhere to the prophetic wisdom and consensus adopt a moderate way regarding the concept of Oneness and of attributes; between disrupting negation and matching analogy.

Similarly, they adopt a moderate way regarding the concept of fate, justice, and actions wavering between fatalism, Jabryyah, and magian fatalism; the concept of names and attributes wavering between those who totally excluded the wrongdoers from being believers like the Kharijites and those who likened the faith of the wicked to the faith of the messengers and supporters of truth like the Murjites and Jahmiyyah; the concept of admonition, reward, and punishment wavering between those who deny the intercession on behalf of the Prophet for the perpetrators of grievous sins and those who deny the admonition enactment altogether like the Murjites; the concept of Imamate, enjoining what is good and forbidding what is evil, wavering between those who approve the sin and transgression of leaders and support the oppressive and those who abstain from offering a helping hand to anyone to promote righteousness and piety: neither in Jihad (the fight for the cause of God), Friday congregation prayer, or feast prayers except for the impeccable, nor do they submit to the Commandments of God and of His Prophet except in submission to a non-existing entity.

The first group treads into the forbidden, while the other drops the obligations of religion and the Islamic code, and the extremists give them up owing to whom they assume oppressive, even if he was perfect in his knowledge and justice.

• CHAPTER 9 •

People of the Right Course .... During Calamity

People of the right course and moderation do their utmost in obeying God and obeying His Prophet; they fear God as much as possible, do their utmost to carry out the Prophet's orders, and do not give up what they had been ordered because others committed what is forbidden. God Almighty says in this regard,

يَا أَيُّهَا الَّذِينَ آمَنُوا عَلَيْكُمْ أَنفُسَكُمْ لَا يَضُرُّكُم مَّن ضَلَّ إِذَا اهْتَدَيْتُمْ (المائدة: 105)

O you who have believed, upon you is [responsibility for] yourselves. Those who have gone astray will not harm you when you have been guided. (Al-Ma'ida: 105)

They do not aid anyone in wrongdoing, eradicate evil with what is eviler, or enjoin good except in good conduct. In fact, they follow a moderate course in all affairs, and so they were described by the Prophet (PBUH) as the saved group that will survive the nation's dissention and division.

One example of a great calamity that befell the Islamic Nation is the Day of Ashoura' when God bestowed martyrdom on the Prophet's grandson, and one of the masters of the youth in Paradise, at the hands of the wicked and the wretched.

Imam Ahmad and others narrated on the authority of Fatima bint al-Hussein, who had witnessed the murder of her father, on the authority of her father al-Hussein ibn Ali, on authority of his grandfather (peace be upon him) that he said, "Whoever is afflicted with a calamity and say whenever he remembers it, however old: 'To God we belong, and to Him we shall return', God will bestow on him the exact reward that he had earned on the first day of affliction." [68]

God had known that the reminiscence of such calamity will be renewed over time, so it was a merit that the narrator of the hadith was the same afflicted person. No doubt that this is a privilege, glory, raising of rank, identification with martyrs, and association with the Prophet's household in enduring various calamities added to the meritorious status of al-Hussein (may God be pleased with him). Al-Hassan and al-Hussein had not experienced the affliction that befell their grandfather, their

THE RIGHTS OF THE PROPHET'S HOUSEHOLD {AHLUL-BAYT}

mother, and their uncle because they were born during the glory and power of Islam and were nurtured by fellow believers, so God honored them with martyrdom; one poisoned, the other murdered. God had stipulated high ranks in His Abode of Dignity, especially for people of affliction, as the Prophet said when asked which people are most severely tested?' He said: 'The Prophets, then the next best and the next best. A person is tested according to his religious commitment. If he is steadfast in his religious commitment, he will be tested more severely, and if he is frail in his religious commitment, he will be tested accordingly. Trials will continue to afflict a person until they leave him walking on the face of the earth with no sin on him.'"[22]

Those who aided in his killing or were satisfied with it are considered from the wretched who participated in his killing. Hence, God had instructed the believers to say upon affliction, however great,

إِنَّا لِلَّهِ وَإِنَّا إِلَيْهِ رَاجِعُونَ (البقرة: 156)

To God we belong, and to Him we shall return (Al-Baqara: 156)

Al-Shafi' narrated in his Musnad (Hadith collection) that when the Prophet died, and his household suffered great affliction, they heard someone saying, "O people of the Prophet's household, God is the Solace in calamities, the

---

[22] Al Turmithe

Compensator for depletion, and the Attainable of the lost. Trust in God and have hope in His Grace, for the one deprived of God's reward is, indeed, the afflicted one."

It is said that they have seen al-khedr[23] offering his condolences at the death of the Prophet.

However, funeral ceremonies are not acknowledged in Islam for neither the Prophet, the predecessors, the successors, the chiefs of the Prophet's household, nor others have offered them.

The killing of Ali as well as the killing of al-Hussein was witnessed by their households and, over the course of time, they had been steadfast in adhering to the Prophet's sunnah. They did not offer funeral ceremonies, nor did they wail aloud; they showed patience, turned to no one else but God for solace as ordained By God and His Prophet, and only gave vent to mild weeping and sadness on the occurrence of the calamity.

The Prophet said, "The manifestation of sadness by the eye and heart is from God; whereas that of the hand and tongue is from the devil."[24]

And added, "Whoever slaps the cheeks, tears the clothes or follows in the footsteps of Jahiliya (Pre-Islamic Dark Ages) is

---

[23] A previous prophet in time of Moses PBUT
[24] Al Suewtie

THE RIGHTS OF THE PROPHET'S HOUSEHOLD {AHLUL-BAYT}

not from us", [25] as when the afflicted laments his loss saying, "What ill-fortune befell me by losing my supporter/ my aid/ my helper!"

He also said, "If the wailing woman does not repent before she dies, she will be made to stand on the Day of Resurrection wearing a shield of itching scabies and a garment of tar."[26]

And said, "God had cursed wailing women together with those who are listening to them." [27]

يَا أَيُّهَا النَّبِيُّ إِذَا جَاءَكَ الْمُؤْمِنَاتُ يُبَايِعْنَكَ عَلَى أَنْ لاَ يُشْرِكْنَ بِاللَّهِ شَيْئًا وَلاَ يَسْرِقْنَ وَلاَ يَزْنِينَ وَلاَ يَقْتُلْنَ أَوْلاَدَهُنَّ وَلاَ يَأْتِينَ بِبُهْتَانٍ يَفْتَرِينَهُ بَيْنَ أَيْدِيهِنَّ وَأَرْجُلِهِنَّ وَلاَ يَعْصِينَكَ فِي مَعْرُوفٍ فَبَايِعْهُنَّ وَاسْتَغْفِرْ لَهُنَّ اللَّهَ إِنَّ اللَّهَ غَفُورٌ رَحِيمٌ (الممتحنة: 12)

O Prophet, when the believing women come to you pledging to you that they will not associate anything with Allah, nor will they steal, nor will they commit unlawful sexual intercourse, nor will they kill their children, nor will they bring forth a slander they have invented between their arms and legs, nor will they disobey you in what is right - then accept their pledge and ask forgiveness for them of Allah. Indeed, Allah is Forgiving and Merciful. (Al mumtahanah : 12)

---

[25] Al Bukhari
[26] Muslim
[27] Musnad Ahmad

The Prophet had explained **'nor will they disobey you in what is right'** that it means wailing aloud.

The Prophet had renounced women who shave their hair or wail loudly (out of grief).

Jarir ibn Abdullah said, "We counted gathering with the household of the deceased and their making food from wailing."

However, it is recommended as sunnah to make food for the household of the deceased because they are preoccupied with their calamity.

The Prophet had paid his condolences for Ja'far ibn Abi talib when he was honored with martyrdom at Mo'tah and said, "Make some food for the household of Ja'far for they are preoccupied with their affliction." [28]

Likewise, the special rituals that some people perform on the Day of Ashoura', like lining the eyelids with kohl, pigmenting the skin or hair, shaking hands, or washing the body, are erroneous innovations that have no origin in religion nor were they mentioned by any prominent scholar.

Like saying, "Whoever washes his body on the Day of Ashoura' will never get sick that year, and whoever lined his eyelids with kohl on the Day of Ashoura' will never be sore-eyed that year."

---

[28] Al Trumithe

THE RIGHTS OF THE PROPHET'S HOUSEHOLD {AHLUL-BAYT}

It is only authorized and authentic that the Prophet had fast on the Day of Ashoura' and instructed Muslims to fast likewise saying, "Fasting this day absolves the wrongdoings of a year."[29]

The Prophet stated that God had rescued Moses and his people, drowned the Pharaoh and his people, and other nations' significant events took place on that day. So, God had honored al-Hussein when he assigned his martyrdom on that very day.

At a certain time, God may assign a person some kind of grace that entails gratitude or some kind of trial that entails patience.

Similarly, the Battle of Badr and the assassination of Ali both occurred on the seventeenth of Ramadan.

Curiously enough, the Prophet was born, migrated, and died on Monday in the month of Rabi' al-Awal.

The believer is sometimes tried with favors that please him, and with evils that upset him simultaneously to teach him to be patient and grateful. So how about when this occurs at two separate times of the same type.

It is recommended to fast on the ninth and tenth of this month, whereas lining the eyelids with kohl is not

---

[29] Musnad Ahmad

recommended. However, the pious who wear it, despite their error, do not mean hostility to the Prophet's household. Whoever meant it or was pleased and content with their calamities is cursed by God, the angels, and all mankind.

In this regard, the Prophet said, "By Him in Whose Hand my life lies; they will not be admitted to the Garden of Paradise until they love you for my sake." [30] This was said when al-Abbas complained that some members of the Quraysh are on bad terms with Beni Hashim.

He also said, "Allah had chosen the Quraysh from Bani Kinanah, and chose Banu Hashim from Quraysh, and chose me from Bani Hashim."[31]

It was also reported that he said, "Love God for His boundless Grace, love me for the love of God, and love my household for my love."[32]

There is much more to say regarding this field.

---

[30] Musnad Ahmad
[31] Muslim
[32] Al Trumithe

• CHAPTER 10 •

Erroneous Innovations and Deviations

The reason for this follow-up was that a brother had presented a paper about the Prophet and the masters of his household, including assigning vows to God in order to witness the arrival of the awaited one. He was pleased and content when the merits and the rights of the Prophet's household were called up. Since this talk can be endless, what was mentioned in this walk was but a fragment of the duties due to them, yet the context could not hold more than what was said.

When he was encountered with questions about lineage and vows to God as instructed by religion, he asked the brothers who came to him to record it in writing. In this regard, the Prophet had said, "Religion is sincere advice." They said, "To whom, O Messenger of Allah?" He said, "To Allah, to His Book, to His

Messenger, to the imams of the Muslims and to their common folk." [33]

As for the paper of lineage and dates, it contained several errors, such as stating that the Prophet died in the month of Safar; that he is Mohammad ibn Abdullah ibn Adul-Mutalib ibn Amr ibn al-Ala'a ibn Hashim, that Ja'far as-Sadiq died during the caliphate of ar-Rashid, and other such errors.

It is acknowledged by the scholars that the Prophet died in the month of Rabi' al-Awal, the same month of his birth and his migration. He died on Monday, the same day of his birth and the descent of God's Revelation. His grandfather is Hashim ibn Abd Manaf; Hashim was casually called Omar or Lofty Amr, as in the poet's saying,

Lofty Amr offered porridge for his folks ....
        when Meccans were suffering hard times

As for Ja'far, the father of Abdullah, he died in 48 hijri during the rule of Abi Ja'far al-Mansour.

As for the awaited one(Al Mahdi), some genealogists specialized in the Prophet's household lineage mentioned that al-Hassan ibn Ali al-Askari died in Askar Samira' without leaving descendants. It was also stated that when his father died in 260

---

[33] Al Bukhari

THE RIGHTS OF THE PROPHET'S HOUSEHOLD {AHLUL-BAYT}

Hijri when he was two years old or a little older, he disappeared since then and became God's argument against mankind and that faith cannot be complete except by believing in him. It was claimed that he was the guided one whom the Prophet heralded his coming and that he knows what the religion falls short of.

In such case, a Muslim should be rigorous in investigating its certainty, asking God for guidance and aid, for God had forbidden tackling matters without knowledge and following in the footsteps of the devil. He had also forbidden saying anything that was contrary to the truth as prescribed by the revealed texts and forbidden following inclinations.

As for the guided (Al Mahdi) one whose harbinger was the Prophet, authorized and trustworthy scholars, the seekers and guardians of sunnah have mentioned him, like Abi Dawud, at-Tirmdhi, Imam Ahmad, and others.

Abdullah ibn Masoud narrated that the Prophet said, "If only one day of this world remained, God would make that day longer, till He sends a man who belongs to my household: whose father's name is the same as my father's, who will fill the earth with equity and justice as it has been filled with oppression and tyranny." [34]

---

[34] Musnad Ahmad and others

In a similar context, Um Salama and others narrated the same meaning of the hadith.

On the authority of Ali ibn Abi Talib that he said, "The guided one is among the descendants of my son," and he pointed to al-Hassan.

The Prophet also said, "At the end of time comes a caliphate who scatters loads of money among people." Authentic hadith.[35]

The Prophet mentioned that his name is Mohammad ibn Abdullah, and not Mohammad ibn al-Hassan. He who said that the father of his grandfather is al-Hussein and that his nickname is al-Hussein Abu Abdullah, has taken the wording out of its context and interpreted it in a Karamita-like fashion.

The Prince of the Faithfull's declaration is unequivocal that he is among al-Hassan's descendants and not al-Hussein, for al-Hassan and al-Hussein resemble Ishmael and Isaac in some aspects, except that the former were not messengers.

The Prophet used to impart God's protection on them by saying, "May the Perfect Words of Allah ward off every devil, every poisonous pest, and every evil eye from you both."[36]

---

[35] Muslim
[36] Al Bukhari

THE RIGHTS OF THE PROPHET'S HOUSEHOLD {AHLUL-BAYT}

And he also said, "Ibrahim, too, used to guard Ishmael and Isaac with these words from harm."

Ishmael was the elder and more forbearing.

Subsequently, the Prophet said while he was on the pulpit, delivering a sermon, "This son of mine is a master and God will make him a means of reconciliation between two major Muslim groups.'[37]

Just like most of the messengers are descendants of Isaac, most of the chief imams are descendants of al-Hussein. And just like the Seal of the Prophets whose teachings transcended and reached the eastern as well as the western regions of the earth was a descendant of Ishmael, the rightly-guided (al mahdi) who will be the last caliphate is a descendant of al-Hassan.

Moreover, in the light of the Qur'an and sunnah, a two-year old child is placed under guardianship for being legally incompetent in handling himself or his wealth until he reaches adulthood. Till then, he is considered an orphan, as God had said,

وَابْتَلُوا الْيَتَامَىٰ حَتَّىٰ إِذَا بَلَغُوا النِّكَاحَ فَإِنْ آنَسْتُم مِّنْهُمْ رُشْدًا فَادْفَعُوا إِلَيْهِمْ أَمْوَالَهُمْ (النساء: 6)

And test the orphans [in their abilities] until they reach marriageable age. Then if you perceive in them sound judgment, release their property to them. [An-Nisa : 6)

---

[37] Al Bukhari

Consequently, how can someone who is too incompetent by the Islamic Law to tackle his own affairs, tackle the affairs of the entire nation?

Or how can he be given leadership over the nation while he remains non-existent? God does not ordain obedience to someone who is inaccessible; four hundred and forty years[38] have elapsed in waiting and he still did not show up, simply because he is non-existent.

Or how could he remain hidden even from his trusted allies and followers and not show up like did his fathers? What justifies such obscure and exclusive disappearance out of all his fathers?

Reasonable people of the past and the present ridicule those who believe in him and claim that their religion will only be complete by believing in him. Such tales encouraged atheists to criticize religion and ridicule the religious who believe in them.

People of knowledge have pinpointed several hypocrites and hidden atheists who allegedly manifest faith in such tales to allure the feeble-minded and the heretics. As a result, falsehoods

---

[38] The Imam refer to his time but as the time of this book being translated in 2018 it is more then 1200 years

THE RIGHTS OF THE PROPHET'S HOUSEHOLD {AHLUL-BAYT}

became rampant —everything is powerless without Allah's support. May God guide this nation to true religion.

Vows to God designated for shrines and mosques:

God has ordained visiting and tending to the houses of worship and performing prayers as much as possible in them and forbidden to establish mosques over graves and cursed whoever does this. God had said,

إِنَّمَا يَعْمُرُ مَسَاجِدَ اللَّهِ مَنْ آمَنَ بِاللَّهِ وَالْيَوْمِ الْآخِرِ وَأَقَامَ الصَّلَاةَ وَآتَى الزَّكَاةَ وَلَمْ يَخْشَ إِلَّا اللَّهَ فَعَسَىٰ أُولَٰئِكَ أَن يَكُونُوا مِنَ الْمُهْتَدِينَ (التوبة: 18)

The mosques of Allah are only to be maintained by those who believe in Allah and the Last Day and establish prayer and give zakah and do not fear except Allah, for it is expected that those will be of the [rightly] guided. (At-Tawba :89)

And said,

وَمَنْ أَظْلَمُ مِمَّن مَّنَعَ مَسَاجِدَ اللَّهِ أَن يُذْكَرَ فِيهَا اسْمُهُ وَسَعَىٰ فِي خَرَابِهَا أُولَٰئِكَ مَا كَانَ لَهُمْ أَن يَدْخُلُوهَا إِلَّا خَائِفِينَ لَهُمْ فِي الدُّنْيَا خِزْيٌ وَلَهُمْ فِي الْآخِرَةِ عَذَابٌ عَظِيمٌ (البقرة: 114)

And who are more unjust than those who prevent the name of Allah from being mentioned in His mosques and strive toward their destruction. It is not for them to enter them except in fear. (Al Baqara:114)

فِي بُيُوتٍ أَذِنَ اللهُ أَن تُرْفَعَ وَيُذْكَرَ فِيهَا اسْمُهُ يُسَبِّحُ لَهُ فِيهَا بِالْغُدُوِّ وَالآصَالِ رِجَالٌ لَا تُلْهِيهِمْ تِجَارَةٌ وَلَا بَيْعٌ عَن ذِكْرِ اللهِ وَإِقَامِ الصَّلَاةِ وَإِيتَاءِ الزَّكَاةِ (النور: 36 -37)

Such niches are] in mosques which Allah has ordered to be raised and that His name be mentioned therein; exalting Him within them in the morning and the evenings [Are] men whom neither commerce nor sale distracts from the remembrance of Allah and performance of prayer and giving of zakah. (Al-Noor : 36-37)

وَأَنَّ الْمَسَاجِدَ لِلَّهِ فَلَا تَدْعُوا مَعَ اللهِ أَحَدًا (الجن: 18)

And [He revealed] that the masjids are for Allah, so do not invoke with Allah anyone. (AL Jin : 18)

وَمَسَاجِدُ يُذْكَرُ فِيهَا اسْمُ اللهِ كَثِيرًا (الحج: 40)

And mosques in which the name of Allah is much mentioned (Al Haj :40)

The Prophet had said, "Whoever builds a mosque for the sake of Allah, Allah will build a house for him in Paradise."[39]

---

[39] Muslim

THE RIGHTS OF THE PROPHET'S HOUSEHOLD {AHLUL-BAYT}

He also said, "Give glad tidings to those who walk to the mosques in the dark, of perfect light on the Day of Resurrection."[40]

The Prophet declared, "Whoever goes to the mosque at dawn or dusk (for Salat), Allah will assign a hospitable abode for him in Paradise, whenever he walks to it or comes back from it."[41]

He explained, "Congregation prayers at the mosque are twenty five times better than praying alone at home or at the market." [42]

And said, "Whoever washed himself thoroughly at home, and then walked to one of the houses of Allah only for the sake of performing an obligatory prayer, one of his steps would obliterate a sin while the other would raise his status." [43]

He expressed, "A Muslim's prayer together with another Muslim is greater in reward than his prayer alone. And a man's prayer with two is greater in reward than his prayer with one; and the more the number, the better favored by Allah." [44]

---

[40] Ibn Majah
[41] Al Bukhari
[42] Al Bukhari
[43] Al Bukhari
[44] Musnad Ahmad and others

"There will be leaders who will delay prayers until past its prescribed time. So observe your prayers on time and count your prayer with them voluntary." [45]

"Your leaders will lead you in prayers. If they conduct it properly, you and they will be rewarded; but if they make mistakes you will earn the reward and they will be held responsible (for the mistakes)."

In fact, this is a voluminous chapter.

He also warned, "God had cursed the Jews for they have transformed the shrines of their prophets to houses of worship." For this reason, the Prophet (PBUH) did not make his grave conspicuous lest it should be taken a mosque. This hadith was said during his illness.

It was five days before the Prophet's death that he was heard saying, "Some predecessors used to transform graves into houses of worship, so beware of transforming your graves to mosques; I forbid you to do that."[46]

When the church of Abyssinia was mentioned, the Prophet said, "Those people used to, whenever a righteous man died, build a place of worship over his grave and adorn it with icons.

---

[45] Muslim
[46] Al Bukhari

THE RIGHTS OF THE PROPHET'S HOUSEHOLD
{AHLUL-BAYT}

Those are the most evil of God's creation on the Day of Resurrection."[47]

All these are authentic traditions in Sihah (authentic hadith collections).

He also narrated, "God had cursed the women who frequent visiting graveyards, those who build mosques over graves, and ornament them with lanterns." [48]

So, how come that the Prophet had cursed those who build mosques over graves and adorn them with lanterns and some Muslim insists on making it an act of obedience and recommendation?

In Sahih Muslim, on the authority of the Prince of the Faithful Ali Ibn Abi Talib that he said, "The Prophet had commissioned me to wipe out conspicuous graves and destroy statues."

It was authorized that the Prophet had said, "O Allah! Do not make my grave an idol set up for worship." [49]

He also said, "Don't make a festivity over my grave, and just pray for me wherever you are for your prayers reach me."[50]

---

[47] Al Bukhari
[48] Al Turmithe
[49] Muwatta Imam Malik
[50] Ibi Dawood

So the Prophet had forbidden the gathering over his grave and that prayers for him are valid wherever a Muslim is regardless of his location.

The previously mentioned hadiths were narrated by the Prophet's household, such as Ali ibn al-Hussein, on the authority of his father, on the authority of his grandfather, Ali; and Abdullah ibn al-Hassan ibn Ali ibn Abi Talib.

They all prohibited erroneous innovations taking place at his grave or any other grave as instructed by the Prophet.

This is the core principle of worshipping idols: preoccupying and dedicating oneself to staying at the graves of the messengers and the righteous and busying oneself with their statues, regardless of the original intention with which they were built.

وَقَالُوا لَا تَذَرُنَّ آلِهَتَكُمْ وَلَا تَذَرُنَّ وَدًّا وَلَا سُوَاعًا وَلَا يَغُوثَ وَيَعُوقَ وَنَسْرًا (نوح: 23)

And said, 'Never leave your gods and never leave Wadd or Suwa' or Yaghuth and Ya'uq and Nasr (Noha : 23)

A group of scholars explained that those idols were originally righteous people; when they died, they built over their graves and carved their statues.

أَفَرَأَيْتُمُ اللَّاتَ وَالْعُزَّىٰ وَمَنَاةَ الثَّالِثَةَ الْأُخْرَىٰ (النجم: 19-20)

THE RIGHTS OF THE PROPHET'S HOUSEHOLD {AHLUL-BAYT}

So have you considered al-Lat and al-'Uzza? And Manat, the third - the other one? (AL Najim : 19-20)

In reference to this verse, Ibn Abbas said, "Al-Lat was a man who used to mix flour with water and offer it to the pilgrims. When he died, they used to gather over his grave. So the Prophet asked God," O Allah! Do not make my grave an idol set up for worship."

He forbade praying at his grave.

That's why when the Muslims built the Prophet's room, they tilted its rear and constructed a small edifice so that no one would pray towards the grave. "Do not sit on the graves or pray towards them," narrated by Muslim.

The Prophet used to go to the people buried at the Baqui', greet them and pray for them.

He taught his Companions to say, on visiting the graves, "Peace be upon the inhabitants of this place among the believers and Muslims and soon will we join you. May Allah have mercy upon those who have preceded us and those who will come after us. May God have mercy on you and guard you. O Allah, do not allure us with temptations after they had passed away. May Allah forgive you and us![51]

---

[51] Muslim

Despite the fact that the Prophet's son, Ibrahim and his daughters Um Kolthoum and Roquayah, and the mistress of all women, Fatima were all buried there, none of them came up with any prohibited acts. What is permissible is to greet them and ask forgiveness for them.

Similarly, regarding the Prophet's share of prayers, he elaborated that praying for him is valid whether close or far away. He said, "Supplicate Allah more often for me on Friday, for your supplications will be displayed before me." He was asked: "O Messenger of Allah! How will our blessings be displayed before you when your body will have decayed?" He replied, "Allah has prohibited earth from touching the bodies of the prophets." [52]

He also stated, "Whoever passes by a grave of a man he had known in his life and greets him, God will retrieve the deceased's soul to his body to answer him."[53]

All such hadiths are authorized by knowledgeable scholars.

Praying and asking for forgiveness reach the deceased whether at his grave or away from it. This is how a Muslim should treat the deceased: praying for them as he used to do in their life.

---

[52] Abi Dawood
[53] Abi Dawood

THE RIGHTS OF THE PROPHET'S HOUSEHOLD {AHLUL-BAYT}

The Prophet had ordered us to pray for him in his life and after his death, and for his household. He, too, instructed us to pray for the believers, men and women, during their life and after their death, at their graves or away from them as well.

He prohibited setting up partners with God, or establishing an edifice for a created being, which is his grave in resemblance to that of God's, which is the Ka'ba. God has enjoined us to travel to it in pilgrimage, set our face towards it during prayer, circumambulate around it, touch its corners, and kiss the black stone which God counted His Right Hand on earth.

Ibn Abbas said, "The Black Stone is God's Right hand on earth; receiving and kissing it simulates saluting and kissing the Hand of God."

The Prophet allowed covering the Ka'ba and hanging curtains over it; whoever clings to them resembles someone clinging to the clothes of his rescuer. It is impermissible to make the houses of created beings on the same level with that of the Creator.

That's why the predecessors prohibited those who visited the grave of the Prophet from kissing it; rather greet him, may my parents be ransomed for him, and pray for him just like the righteous predecessors used to.

If the predecessors (AL Salaf) who were more knowledgeable with God's religion, the sunnah and the rights of

His Prophet, the rights of the former and later generations of his household did not commit any of the erroneous innovations that is categorized under polytheism and idolatry because God had forbidden them to do so. Instead, they worshipped only God while setting no other partner with Him, were sincere in their religion as ordained by God and His Messenger, tended to the houses of God through performing their prayers, reciting Qur'an, remembering God, and supplicating.

Hence, it is unfathomable for a Muslim to forsake the Book of God, the teachings of His Prophet PBUH, and the path of the believers' predecessors and follow what some people erroneously innovated in religion, whether willfully or by mistake.

The bearer of this book was told that a Muslim should not support the false novelties opposing the Divine Revelation and sunnah that are found over the graves of the messengers, the chiefs of the Prophet's household, and the scholars, in case these graves were authentic. How about that most of them are fake graves!

Vows to God assigned to these graves are considered transgressions forbidden by God, His Prophet, and the predecessors. The Prophet said, "Whoever vows to God in obedience, let him carry out his vow; whoever vows to disobey Him, let him not."[54]

THE RIGHTS OF THE PROPHET'S HOUSEHOLD {AHLUL-BAYT}

He said, "The absolution of a vow to God is the absolution of common oath," narrated in Sihah.[55]

If the vow was in obedience to God and His Messenger, like vowing to pray, fast, perform pilgrimage, or donate in charity, it should be fulfilled. However, if the vow was made in disobedience whether involving disbelief or not, like assigning vows to the idols in India, or like the vows the idolaters used to assign to their idols, such as al-Lat which was in Ta'if, al-Uzza which was in Arafa near Mecca, and Manat in Medina.

These three cities were in Hijaz. Their people used to assign their vows to their alleged deities and worship them thinking that they would bring them nearer to God in order to fulfill their needs. In this context, God had said,

مَا نَعْبُدُهُمْ إِلاَّ لِيُقَرِّبُونَا إِلَى اللهِ زُلْفَىٰ (الزمر: 3)

We only worship them that they may bring us nearer to Allah in position (Al Zimar : 3)

Under such transgression fall the vows that some ignorant Muslims assign to a water spring, a well, a water channel, a cave, a stone, a tree, a grave even if it is a messenger's or a righteous person's, or allocate oil, wax, a covering, gold, or

---

[54] Al Bukhari
[55] Muslim

silver in binding vows to such things. All such binding vows are made in disobedience and ought not be fulfilled.

Some scholars argue that the absolution for binding vows is like that of common oaths. The Prophet said, "No binding vows should be made in disobedience, and their absolution resembles that of a common oath."

It was reported in the Sahih, "Binding vows are pardoned like common oaths."[56]

However, if those binding vows are assigned to lawful and recommended acts like when grease is allocated to illuminate mosques, or money and clothes allocated for the needy people of Muslims, the Prophet's household, and common believers, or other acts that are prescribed by God and His messenger.

Should a handful of ignorant people assume that these prohibited vows fulfilled his wishes, brought about some benefit like money or wellness, or warded off some evil like enemies or the like, then they are definitely misled.

The Prophet PBUH had forbidden binding vows and said, "It's of no benefit, but is extracted from the miserly."[57]

---

[56] Al Bukhari
[57] Al Bukhari and others

THE RIGHTS OF THE PROPHET'S HOUSEHOLD {AHLUL-BAYT}

So, he counted binding vows amongst the disliked actions. However fulfilling them are required provided they are made in obedience to God and His messenger.

It was reported, in different contexts, that the Prophet said that binding vows are of no avail except that they are extracted from the miserly in case it is made in obedience. But it is impermissible to fulfill them in case they involved transgression.

As Islam is firmly established and well-grounded and people are preoccupied with visiting the graves of the righteous and of the Prophet's household, people have to obey God and His Messenger, follow in the footsteps of true religion, and cease to permit what is impermissible. God had sent His messengers and revealed His Books so that all submission and worship are assigned to God alone.

God had said,

وَاسْأَلْ مَنْ أَرْسَلْنَا مِن قَبْلِكَ مِن رُسُلِنَا أَجَعَلْنَا مِن دُونِ الرَّحْمَٰنِ آلِهَةً يُعْبَدُونَ (الزخرف: 45)

And ask those We sent before you of Our messengers; have We made besides the Most Merciful deities to be worshipped? (Az-Zukhruf : 45)

And said,

شَرَعَ لَكُم مِّنَ الدِّينِ مَا وَصَّىٰ بِهِ نُوحًا وَالَّذِي أَوْحَيْنَا إِلَيْكَ وَمَا وَصَّيْنَا بِهِ إِبْرَاهِيمَ وَمُوسَىٰ وَعِيسَىٰ أَنْ أَقِيمُوا الدِّينَ وَلَا تَتَفَرَّقُوا فِيهِ كَبُرَ عَلَى الْمُشْرِكِينَ مَا تَدْعُوهُمْ إِلَيْهِ اللَّهُ يَجْتَبِي إِلَيْهِ مَن يَشَاءُ وَيَهْدِي إِلَيْهِ مَن يُنِيبُ (الشورى: 13)

He has ordained for you of religion what He enjoined upon Noah and that which We have revealed to you, [O Muhammad], and what We enjoined upon Abraham and Moses and Jesus - to establish the religion and not be divided therein. Difficult for those who associate others with Allah is that to which you invite them. Allah chooses for Himself whom He wills and guides to Himself whoever turns back [to Him]. (Ash-Shura : 13)

He affirmed,

وَلَقَدْ بَعَثْنَا فِي كُلِّ أُمَّةٍ رَّسُولًا أَنِ اعْبُدُوا اللَّهَ وَاجْتَنِبُوا الطَّاغُوتَ فَمِنْهُم مَّنْ هَدَى اللَّهُ وَمِنْهُم مَّنْ حَقَّتْ عَلَيْهِ الضَّلَالَةُ فَسِيرُوا فِي الْأَرْضِ فَانظُرُوا كَيْفَ كَانَ عَاقِبَةُ الْمُكَذِّبِينَ (النحل: 36)

And We certainly sent into every nation a messenger, [saying], "Worship Allah and avoid Taghut." And among them were those whom Allah guided, and among them were those upon whom error was [deservedly] decreed. So proceed through the earth and observe how was the end of the deniers. (An-Nahl: 36)

He speaks of those who take the angels and messengers as deities with God,

قُلِ ادْعُوا الَّذِينَ زَعَمْتُم مِّن دُونِهِ فَلَا يَمْلِكُونَ كَشْفَ الضُّرِّ عَنكُمْ وَلَا تَحْوِيلًا (الاسراء: 56

THE RIGHTS OF THE PROPHET'S HOUSEHOLD {AHLUL-BAYT}

Say, "Invoke those you have claimed [as gods] besides Him, for they do not possess the [ability for] removal of adversity from you or [for its] transfer [to someone else]." (Al-Isra' : 56

He also stated,

وَلَا يَأْمُرَكُمْ أَن تَتَّخِذُوا الْمَلَائِكَةَ وَالنَّبِيِّينَ أَرْبَابًا أَيَأْمُرُكُم بِالْكُفْرِ بَعْدَ إِذْ أَنتُم مُّسْلِمُونَ (آل عمران: 80)

Nor could he order you to take the angels and prophets as lords. Would he order you to disbelief after you had been Muslims? (Ali Imran : 80)

God answered those who took deities to intercede to God on behalf of them,

أَمِ اتَّخَذُوا مِن دُونِ اللَّهِ شُفَعَاءَ قُلْ أَوَلَوْ كَانُوا لَا يَمْلِكُونَ شَيْئًا وَلَا يَعْقِلُونَ قُل لِّلَّهِ الشَّفَاعَةُ جَمِيعًا لَّهُ مُلْكُ السَّمَاوَاتِ وَالْأَرْضِ ثُمَّ إِلَيْهِ تُرْجَعُونَ وَإِذَا ذُكِرَ اللَّهُ وَحْدَهُ اشْمَأَزَّتْ قُلُوبُ الَّذِينَ لَا يُؤْمِنُونَ بِالْآخِرَةِ وَإِذَا ذُكِرَ الَّذِينَ مِن دُونِهِ إِذَا هُمْ يَسْتَبْشِرُونَ قُلِ اللَّهُمَّ فَاطِرَ السَّمَاوَاتِ وَالْأَرْضِ عَالِمَ الْغَيْبِ وَالشَّهَادَةِ أَنتَ تَحْكُمُ بَيْنَ عِبَادِكَ فِي مَا كَانُوا فِيهِ يَخْتَلِفُونَ (الزمر: 43-46)

Or have they taken other than Allah as intercessors? Say, "Even though they do not possess [power over] anything, nor do they reason?" Say, "To Allah belongs [the right to allow] intercession entirely. To Him belongs the dominion of the heavens and the earth. Then to Him you will be returned." And when Allah is mentioned alone, the hearts of those who do not believe in the Hereafter shrink with aversion, but when those [worshipped] other than Him are mentioned, immediately they rejoice. Say, "O Allah, Creator of the heavens and the earth, Knower of the unseen and the witnessed, You will judge between your servants concerning that over which they used to differ." (Az-Zumar : 43-36)

He declared,

اتَّخَذُوا أَحْبَارَهُمْ وَرُهْبَانَهُمْ أَرْبَابًا مِّن دُونِ اللَّهِ وَالْمَسِيحَ ابْنَ مَرْيَمَ وَمَا أُمِرُوا إِلَّا لِيَعْبُدُوا إِلَهًا وَاحِدًا لَا إِلَهَ إِلَّا هُوَ سُبْحَانَهُ عَمَّا يُشْرِكُونَ (التوبة: 31)

They have taken their scholars and monks as lords besides Allah, and [also] the Messiah, the son of Mary. And they were not commanded except to worship one God; there is no deity except Him. Exalted is He above whatever they associate with Him. (At-Tawba :31)

He also asserted,

مَن ذَا الَّذِي يَشْفَعُ عِندَهُ إِلَّا بِإِذْنِهِ (البقرة: 255)

Who is it that can intercede with Him except by His permission? (Al-Baqara : 255)

وَكَم مِّن مَّلَكٍ فِي السَّمَاوَاتِ لَا تُغْنِي شَفَاعَتُهُمْ شَيْئًا إِلَّا مِن بَعْدِ أَن يَأْذَنَ اللَّهُ لِمَن يَشَاءُ وَيَرْضَىٰ (النجم: 26)

And how many angels there are in the heavens whose intercession will not avail at all except [only] after Allah has permitted [it] to whom He wills and approves. (An-Najm : 26)

وَلَا يَشْفَعُونَ إِلَّا لِمَنِ ارْتَضَىٰ (الأنبياء: 28)

THE RIGHTS OF THE PROPHET'S HOUSEHOLD {AHLUL-BAYT}

And they cannot intercede except on behalf of one whom He approves. (Al-Anbiya : 28)

He said,

وَلاَ تَنفَعُ الشَّفَاعَةُ عِندَهُ إِلاَّ لِمَنْ أَذِنَ لَهُ (سبأ: 23)

And intercession does not benefit with Him except for one whom He permits. (Saba:25)

All Revelations of God, from first to last, reassure that all submission and true religion should be dedicated to God alone, particularly the book that has descended on Prophet Mohammad from on high and his teachings which completed religion.

In this regard, God says,

الْيَوْمَ أَكْمَلْتُ لَكُمْ دِينَكُمْ (المائدة: 3)

This day I have perfected for you your religion (Al-ma'ida:3)

And says,

ثُمَّ جَعَلْنَاكَ عَلَىٰ شَرِيعَةٍ مِّنَ الْأَمْرِ فَاتَّبِعْهَا وَلَا تَتَّبِعْ أَهْوَاءَ الَّذِينَ لَا يَعْلَمُونَ (الجاثية: 18)

Then We put you, [O Muhammad], on an ordained way concerning the matter [of religion]; so follow it and do not follow the inclinations of those who do not know. (Al-Jathiya:18)

The essence of faith is sincerity to God and exacting justice in all walks of life

قُلْ أَمَرَ رَبِّي بِالْقِسْطِ وَأَقِيمُوا وُجُوهَكُمْ عِندَ كُلِّ مَسْجِدٍ وَادْعُوهُ مُخْلِصِينَ لَهُ الدِّينَ كَمَا بَدَأَكُمْ تَعُودُونَ فَرِيقًا هَدَىٰ وَفَرِيقًا حَقَّ عَلَيْهِمُ الضَّلَالَةُ (الأعراف: 29-30)

Say, [O Muhammad], "My Lord has ordered justice and that you maintain yourselves [in worship of Him] at every place [or time] of prostration, and invoke Him, sincere to Him in religion." Just as He originated you, you will return [to life] - A group [of you] He guided, and a group deserved [to be in] error. (Al-A'raf : 29-30)

The Prophet had filtered religion from associating any partners with God, tiny or immense. He said, "Whoever vows by anything but Allah has associated partners with Him," narrated by at-Tirmidhi.

He also warned, "God had forbidden that you swear by your fathers. Whoever vows, let him swear by God or keep silent," a well-known hadith in Sihah.[58]

He said, "Never say what God wills and Mohammad; rather say what God wills and then Mohammad."[59]

A man addressed him saying, "By God's will and yours." The Prophet reprimanded him saying, "Have you associated me partner with God? Rather say, 'By God's will alone.'"[60]

---

[58] Musnad Ahmad
[59] Musnad Ahmad and others
[60] Musnad Ahmad

THE RIGHTS OF THE PROPHET'S HOUSEHOLD
{AHLUL-BAYT}

It was reported that he said, "In this nation's religion, associating partners with God is more subtle than the footfalls of ants."[61]

He also said that the ostentatious actions meant to impress people fall under associating partners with God.

قُلْ إِنَّمَا أَنَا بَشَرٌ مِّثْلُكُمْ يُوحَىٰ إِلَيَّ أَنَّمَا إِلَٰهُكُمْ إِلَٰهٌ وَاحِدٌ ۖ فَمَن كَانَ يَرْجُو لِقَاءَ رَبِّهِ فَلْيَعْمَلْ عَمَلًا صَالِحًا وَلَا يُشْرِكْ بِعِبَادَةِ رَبِّهِ أَحَدًا (الكهف: 110)

Say, "I am only a man like you, to whom has been revealed that your god is one God. So whoever would hope for the meeting with his Lord - let him do righteous work and not associate in the worship of his Lord anyone." (Al-Kahf:110)

He taught his Companions to say, "O Allah! I seek refuge in You that I should associate partners with You while I know, and ask Your forgiveness for what I do not know."

Similarly, the giver and the recipient of charity, who do not assign their donations for the sake of God and say, "for the sake of so and so, referring to some Companions or members of the Prophet's household, until demanding charity on their behalf becomes a justification to devour people's wealth unjustly, are committing dubious actions. So, a handful of people who claim to abide by sunnah give others while, in fact, the devil has the

---

[61] Musnad Ahmad

upper hand over them all. Charity and other religious deeds are only allowed to be offered for the sake of God.

God had said,

وَسَيُجَنَّبُهَا الأَتْقَى الَّذِي يُؤْتِي مَالَهُ يَتَزَكَّىٰ وَمَا لِأَحَدٍ عِندَهُ مِن نِّعْمَةٍ تُجْزَىٰ إِلَّا ابْتِغَاءَ وَجْهِ رَبِّهِ الْأَعْلَىٰ وَلَسَوْفَ يَرْضَىٰ (الليل: 17-21)

But the righteous one will avoid it [He] who gives [from] his wealth to purify himself And not [giving] for anyone who has [done him] a favor to be rewarded. But only seeking the countenance of his Lord, Most High And he is going to be satisfied. (Al-Lail: 17-21)

And said,

وَمَا آتَيْتُم مِّن زَكَاةٍ تُرِيدُونَ وَجْهَ اللَّهِ فَأُولَٰئِكَ هُمُ الْمُضْعِفُونَ (الروم: 39)

But what you give in zakah, desiring the countenance of Allah - those are the multipliers. (Ar-Rum:39)

And,

وَمَثَلُ الَّذِينَ يُنفِقُونَ أَمْوَالَهُمُ ابْتِغَاءَ مَرْضَاتِ اللَّهِ وَتَثْبِيتًا مِّنْ أَنفُسِهِمْ كَمَثَلِ جَنَّةٍ بِرَبْوَةٍ أَصَابَهَا وَابِلٌ فَآتَتْ أُكُلَهَا ضِعْفَيْنِ فَإِن لَّمْ يُصِبْهَا وَابِلٌ فَطَلٌّ (البقرة: 265)

And the example of those who spend their wealth seeking means to the approval of Allah and assuring [reward for] themselves is like a garden on high ground which is hit by a downpour - so it yields its fruits in double. And [even] if it is not hit by a downpour, then a drizzle [is sufficient]. (Al-Baqara : 265)

THE RIGHTS OF THE PROPHET'S HOUSEHOLD
{AHLUL-BAYT}

وَيُطْعِمُونَ الطَّعَامَ عَلَىٰ حُبِّهِ مِسْكِينًا وَيَتِيمًا وَأَسِيرًا إِنَّمَا نُطْعِمُكُمْ لِوَجْهِ اللَّهِ لَا نُرِيدُ مِنكُمْ جَزَاءً وَلَا شُكُورًا (الانسان: 8-9)

And they give food in spite of love for it to the needy, the orphan, and the captive, [Saying], "We feed you only for the countenance of Allah. We wish not from you reward or gratitude. (Al-Insan:8-9)

وَمَا تَفَرَّقَ الَّذِينَ أُوتُوا الْكِتَابَ إِلَّا مِن بَعْدِ مَا جَاءَتْهُمُ الْبَيِّنَةُ وَمَا أُمِرُوا إِلَّا لِيَعْبُدُوا اللَّهَ مُخْلِصِينَ لَهُ الدِّينَ حُنَفَاءَ وَيُقِيمُوا الصَّلَاةَ وَيُؤْتُوا الزَّكَاةَ وَذَٰلِكَ دِينُ الْقَيِّمَةِ (البينة: 4-5)

Nor did those who were given the Scripture become divided until after there had come to them clear evidence. And they were not commanded except to worship Allah, [being] sincere to Him in religion, inclining to truth, and to establish prayer and to give zakah. And that is the correct religion.(Al-Bayyina:4-5)

For His worship, God had enjoined prayer that includes supplication and God's remembrance, alms-giving and charity of various kinds: food, clothes, money, etc.

May God make our faith and that of the believers true and sincere, worship Him alone, hold tight to His Book and to the firm rope of religion, benefit from His Revelation and Wisdom, turn away the devils of mankind and Jinn from us, protect us from deviations off His Path, guide us to the righteous path with those upon whom Allah has bestowed His favor of the prophets, the steadfast affirmers of truth, the martyrs and the righteous. And excellent are those as companions.

IBN TAYMIYYAH

Praise be to God, the Lord of all the worlds; peace and blessings be upon Prophet Mohammad and his kinsfolk.

ABOUT THE AUTHOR

Taqī ad-Dīn Ahmad ibn Taymiyyah, known as Ibn Taymiyyah born in 1263 AD, one of the most Famous Muslim scholars.

Had a wide knowledge in different subject and strong views base on Islamic source and sunnah Tradition..

Printed in Great Britain
by Amazon